Valdez Alaska Trumpeter Swans

Valdez Alaska Trumpeter Swans

Rearing Five Cygnets

BOB BENDA

ISBN: 1519561423
ISBN 13: 9781519561428

I have been able to observe and photograph a pair of Trumpeter Swans for many years. They return every year to the same pond near the Richardson Highway in Valdez, Alaska. They have produced young swans called cygnets every year. They usually had 1 to 4 cygnets, but one year they successfully reared 5 cygnets. I will use my photos to tell their story from rebuilding the nest in the spring to leaving the pond in the fall. This photo shows the Trumpeter Swans in late April when they returned to the pond. The pond was still partially frozen, snow covered, with only a few areas of open water. This photo shows the male and female swans in one of the open water areas.

The female swan is walking on the ice toward the old nest. The swans reuse this nest each year. They have to rebuild the nest each year after the snow melts off.

She walked from the ice onto the old nest. The swan pair will start to rebuild the nest so it's ready for egg laying and incubation.

The female swan starts rebuilding the old nest. The male swan is standing on the ice watching her. They will both work to rebuild the old nest.

The ice and snow has melted off the pond. The swans mated and the female swan laid her eggs. She's incubating them now. The male is gathering material to add to the nest. It takes about 32 to 37 days for the eggs to hatch. When the female leaves the nest to feed she will cover the eggs or the male swan will incubate the eggs while she's feeding.

The eggs have hatched and there are five cygnets. Mom and dad are grooming their feathers. The cygnets are lying in the nest. They have down feathers now and will try grooming them. I don't know if grooming is an instinct or if they learn by watching their parents.

The parents and cygnets leave the nest several times each day to feed on vegetation. The mom and dad keep close to the cygnets to protect them from predators. Bald eagles roost in trees near the pond and try to prey on the cygnets. The adult swans flap their wings when the eagles fly toward the cygnets.

The adults and cygnets are feeding on plants in the pond. The cygnets are small in early June, but they will grow rapidly as summer progresses.

This photo was taken in early July. Mom and one cygnet are in the grass by the nest. The other cygnets are starting to follow them. You can see how fast the cygnets grew in three weeks. They are starting to lose their down feathers and actively walk around the nest. Trumpeter swan nests are round shaped and can be 4 to 12 feet (1.2 to 3.6 meters) in diameter.

The cygnets follow mom to an area to feed. Dad is following behind them. When the cygnets are young the parents and cygnets usually swim in a line like this.

After feeding they return to the nest to rest. Four cygnets are resting and one is flexing its wings. Dad is drying his wings after he groomed his feathers. Mom is feeding in the water.

Three of the cygnets are now exercising their wings. Mom and dad are both feeding.

This is later in July. Two of the cygnets and mom have left the nest and are in the water. The other three cygnets are getting ready to follow them. They are leaving the nest to feed.

They are feeding on seeds from the emergent vegetation. I don't know how many times they leave the nest to feed each day, but the cygnets grow rapidly and need plenty of food to grow. They will fledge in 3 to 4 months after hatching and leave the pond.

The adult swans bathe in the pond. They do this regularly and groom their feathers after bathing. During the summer the adults molt and replace their flight feathers.

Mom and dad have finished bathing, grooming, and drying their feathers. Now the cygnets try bathing like their mom and dad.

When the cygnets were smaller the adults and cygnets always stayed together. One day I saw dad with three cygnets, but I didn't see mom and the other two cygnets. I looked around pond, but couldn't find them.

Dad and the three cygnets seemed to be looking for mom and the other two cygnets.

Dad and the three cygnets swam to the lower part of the pond and found mom and the other two cygnets. Both adults had their wings raised and seemed to be honking at each other. Maybe they were blaming each other for going the wrong way.

Dad and mom were still honking at each other. I could hear them from where I was taking their pictures. I'm sure the cygnets were wondering what was going on.

Mom and dad seemed to have calmed down. They looked like they were going to take the cygnets back to the nest the same route they took to the lower pond.

Dad led his three cygnets back the way they came from the upper pond. Mom decided to follow them with her two cygnets. It seems the family dispute was over.

Here they are all together swimming to the upper pond. They returned to the nest to rest.

This is mid-August. You can see how much the cygnets have grown two months after they hatched. They have shed their down feathers and grown new feathers. The parents have finished molting their flight feathers. Now the adults will start teaching the cygnets to fly so they can all leave the pond.

It is early September and the cygnets are learning to fly. The adults and three cygnets are feeding. One of the cygnets is flapping its wings practicing flying.

All five of the cygnets are practicing flapping their wings. The cygnet on the top of the photo is practicing the running takeoff swans use. You can see where its feet splash on the water.

Here is the adult swan and one of the cygnets feeding on vegetation in the pond. You can see how much the cygnet grew compared to the adult.

This is how one of the adults feeds on submerged plant material in the pond. You can see its large paddle-like feet. When swans take off to fly they use their feet to run on the water. They may need up to 100 yards (32 meters) space to lift off.

Since the pond is too small to allow the swans to fly they have to leave the pond in order to actually fly. To leave the pond they have to cross the highway. They then swim in a tributary to the Lowe River. The Lowe River is where they practice takeoffs, landings, and flying. This photo shows them returning one afternoon on the tributary. I never did get a photo of them leaving the pond.

The swans reach the bank alongside the two lane highway. They'll have to cross the highway again to reach the pond.

The adults and cygnets cross the highway to return to the pond. They do this trip daily for one or two weeks. When the cygnets are able to fly the swans will abandon the pond.

The adult swans and cygnets left the pond and flew to nearby Robe Lake. They spent late summer and early fall feeding on this lake.

Sometimes the swans would leave Robe Lake and fly elsewhere around Valdez. Here they are feeding in the wetlands along the ocean.

Here is a good example of how the adults and cygnets run on the water before they become airborne. You can see the water splashes where their feet hit the water.

They're flying over the Lowe River. They are probably flying back to Robe Lake. If you count the swans you can see there are seven. The cygnets are starting to lose some of their grey color in their wings. They will be all white feathered next year. They will not form pair bonds and start breeding until their 5th to 7th year. Trumpeter swans often mate for life and stay together year round.

Here is dad and two cygnets at Robe Lake in late October. You can see how much the cygnets grew the past two months.

Here's one of the cygnets in shallow water. It's grooming itself. It is still mostly grey in color.

Now it's scratching its head. You can see how big its foot is in this photo.

You can see how large its wingspan is as it dries its wings. You can also see the wing feathers are starting to turn white.

The sun is setting in Valdez in early November. We are down to about 8 daylight hours this time of year. Mom, dad, and the five cygnets were eating their evening meal. I hope you enjoyed their story.

Alaska Trumpeter Swan Fact Sheet

1. The trumpeter swan is the heaviest living bird native to North America
2. Adults measure 138-165 cm (4 ft 6 in-5 ft 5 in) though large males can exceed 180 cm (5 ft 11 in) in total length
3. The weight of adult birds is typically 7-13.6 kg (15-30 lb)
4. Trumpeter swans are one of the heaviest birds capable of flight
5. Its wing span ranges from 185 to 250 cm (6 ft 1 in to 8 ft 2 in)
6. They breed in large shallow ponds, undisturbed lakes, wetlands, and wide slow rivers
7. The largest numbers of breeding pairs are found in Alaska
8. Their diet is almost entirely aquatic plants. They will eat leaves and stems of submerged and emergent plants.
9. The young feed on insects, fish eggs, small fish and crustaceans along with plants. When they are a few months old they change to a vegetation-based diet
10. Trumpeter swans often mate for life
11. Both parents participate in raising the young
12. Most bond pairs are formed when swans are 4 to 7 years old
13. Egg laying occurs between April and May
14. The female lays 3-12 eggs with 4 to 6 being average

15. The same nesting location will be used for several years
16. Both parents help build the nest
17. The nest is a mound of vegetation on a small island. It ranges in size from 1.2 m to 3.6 m (3.9 to 11.8 ft) The larger size is for nests used repeatedly
18. Egg incubation is 32-37 days. The female does most of the incubating, but the male will also incubate the eggs
19. The cygnets (young swans) can swim within two days and feed themselves within a week
20. Cygnets fledge (fly) after 3 to 4 months
21. Adults molt in the summer when they temporarily lose their flight feathers
22. In captivity trumpeter swans have survived to 33 years old. In the wild they have lived to at least 24 years
23. Young trumpeter swans may have as little as a 40% chance of survival
24. When their eggs and young are threatened by predators the parents are very aggressive. They bob their heads, hiss and may attack a predator with beating wings and a thrusting beak
25. The male swan is called a Cob and the female swan is called a Pen. The young are called Cygnets
26. More information can be found at http://en.wikipedia.org/wiki/Trumpeter_swan

www.ingramcontent.com/pod-product-compliance
Lightning Source LLC
Chambersburg PA
CBHW050755290526
45792CB00008B/2189